Festivals

My Rosh Hashanah

Monica Hughes

Little Nippers

www.heinemann.co.uk/library
Visit our website to find out more information about **Heinemann Library** books.

To order:
☎ Phone 44 (0) 1865 888066
▤ Send a fax to 44 (0) 1865 314091
▭ Visit the Heinemann Bookshop at www.heinemann.co.uk/library to browse our catalogue and order online.

Editorial: Sarah Eason and Georga Godwin
Design: Jo Hinton-Malivoire and Tokay, Bicester, UK (www.tokay.co.uk)
Picture Research: Rosie Garai
Production: Séverine Ribierre

Originated by Dot Gradations Ltd
Printed and bound in China by South China Printing Company

ISBN 0 431 18634 0 (hardback)
07 06 05 04 03
10 9 8 7 6 5 4 3 2 1

ISBN 0 431 18640 5 (paperback)
07 06 05 04 03
10 9 8 7 6 5 4 3 2 1

British Library Cataloguing in Publication Data
Hughes, Monica
Little Nippers Festivals My Rosh Hashanah
296.4'315
A full catalogue record for this book is available from the British Library.

Acknowledgements
The Publishers would like to thank Chris Schwarz and Corbis/Richard T. Nowitz **p. 23** for permission to reproduce photographs.

Cover photograph of the children learning about Abraham and Isaac, reproduced with permission of Chris Schwarz.

The Publishers would like to thank the family and school involved and Philip Emmett for their assistance in the preparation of this book.

Every effort has been made to contact copyright holders of any material reproduced in this book. Any omissions will be rectified in subsequent printings if notice is given to the Publishers.

Contents

3

Learning about Rosh Hashanah

I listen carefully to the story
of Abraham and Isaac.

In the kitchen

I help Mummy make two round challah loaves.

7

A special meal

Here come the challah loaves.

The table is set for our special meal.

Rosh Hashanah blessings

Mummy **lights** the candles very carefully.

Soon it will be my turn
to take a sip of wine.

Apples and honey

I helped to slice the apples.

A new day, a new year

The shofar is blown all over the world.

A walk by the sea

We enjoy being out in the
fresh air after our meal.

Look, the sea is taking the crumbs away.

23

Index

The end

Notes for adults

Most festivals and celebrations share common elements that will be familiar to the young child, such as new clothes, special food, sending and receiving cards and presents, giving to charity, being with family and friends and a busy and exciting build-up time. It is important that the child has an opportunity to compare and contrast their own experiences with those of the children in the book. This will be helped by asking the child open-ended questions, using phrases like: What do you remember about …? What did we do …? Where did we go …? Who did we see …? How did you feel …?

Rosh Hashanah is one of the most important Jewish festivals. Special services are held at the synagogue lead by the Rabbi and a shofar, rams horn, is blown one hundred times. It is a New Year celebration that takes place over two days in September or October. Traditionally, apples are dipped in honey and eaten, and crumbs are thrown into moving water as a way of casting away sins so each person starts the New Year with a clean slate.

Follow up activities could include making a Rosh Hashanah card for a Jewish friend, finding a children's version of the story of Abraham and Isaac, trying some apple dipped in honey for themselves and making a list of all the special things the children do in the book.